S0-AYI-732

WITHDRAWN

Maria Edgeworth

THE IRISH WRITERS SERIES
James F. Carens, General Editor

FRANCIS STUART	J. H. Natterstad
PATRICK KAVANAGH	Darcy O'Brien
BRINSLEY MACNAMARA AND GEORGE SHIELS	Raymond J. Porter
STEPHEN MACKENNA	Roger Rosenblatt
JACK B. YEATS	Robin Skelton
WILLIAM ALLINGHAM	Alan Warner
SAMUEL LOVER	Mabel Worthington
FLANN O'BRIEN	Bernard Benstock
DENIS JOHNSTON	James F. Carens
WILLIAM LARMINIE	Richard J. Finneran
SIR SAMUEL FERGUSON	Malcolm Brown
LADY GREGORY	Hazard Adams
GEORGE RUSSELL (AE)	Richard M. Kain and James O'Brien
DION BOUCICAULT	Peter A. Tasch
THOMAS DAVIS	Eileen Ibarra
LOUIS MACNEICE	Christopher Armitage
PADRAIC COLUM	Charles Burgess

MARIA EDGEWORTH

James Newcomer

Lewisburg
BUCKNELL UNIVERSITY PRESS

© 1973 by Associated University Presses
Associated University Presses, Inc.
Cranbury, New Jersey 08512

Library of Congress Cataloging in Publication Data

Newcomer, James.
    Maria Edgeworth.

    (The Irish writers series)
    Bibliography: p.
1. Edgeworth, Maria, 1767–1849.
PR4646.N42   823′.7   77-125886
ISBN 0-8387-7761-9
ISBN 0-8387-7732-5 (pbk.)

PR
4646
.N42

Printed in the United States of America

Contents

Chronology

1767   (January 1) Birth of Maria Edgeworth (The year 1767 has been accepted for 200 years, but recent scholarship gives 1768.)

1773   Death of Maria's mother
Marriage of Mr. Edgeworth to Honora Sneyd

1773–1775   In Ireland

1780   Death of her stepmother, Honora
Marriage of Mr. Edgeworth to Elizabeth Sneyd

1782   Removal of the Edgeworths to Ireland

1791–1792   Visit to England (All her visits to England and the Continent are listed as occasions that extended her knowledge of the world.)

1795   *Letters for Literary Ladies*

1796   *The Parent's Assistant*

1797   Death of her stepmother, Elizabeth

1798   *Practical Education*
Marriage of Mr. Edgeworth to Frances Beaufort

1799   *A Rational Primer*
Visit to England

1800   *Castle Rackrent*

1801   *Harry and Lucy* Parts I and II ⎫
       Rosamond Parts I, II, III   ⎬ *Early Lessons* in
       Frank Parts I, II, III, IV   ⎪ six volumes
       The Little Dog Trusty ⎭
       Moral Tales in five volumes
       Belinda

1802   *Essay on Irish Bulls*

1802–1803   Visit to England, Belgium, France, Scotland; stay in Paris
       Proposal by Chevalier Edelcrantz

1804   *Popular Tales*

1805   *The Modern Griselda*

1806   *Leonora*

1809   *Essays on Professional Education*
       Ennui ⎫
       Madame de Fleury ⎪
       Almeria ⎬ *Tales of Fashionable Life,*
       The Dun ⎪ first set,
       Manoeuvring ⎭ in three volumes

1812   *Vivian* ⎫
       The Absentee ⎬ *Tales of Fashionable Life,*
       Emilie de Coulanges ⎭ second set,
               in three volumes

1813   Visit to England

1814   *Continuation of Early Lessons*
       Patronage
       Return of Lovell Edgeworth after years of captivity in France

1816   *Readings on Poetry*

1817   *Harrington*
       Ormond

Comic Dramas (three plays)
Death of Richard Lovell Edgeworth
1818–1819 Visit to England
1820 *Memoirs of Richard Lovell Edgeworth*
Visit to England, France, Switzerland
1821 *Rosamond: A Sequel to Early Lessons*
1821–1822 Visit to England
1822 *Frank: A Sequel to Frank in Early Lessons*
1823 Visit to Sir Walter Scott in Scotland
1825 *Harry and Lucy Concluded* in four volumes
Visit by Sir Walter Scott to Edgeworthstown
1826 Takes over management of estate from Lovell
1827 *Little Plays* (three plays for children)
1830–1831 Visit to England
1832 *Garry Owen* and *Poor Bob the Chimney Sweeper*
1833 Tour of Connemara
1834 *Helen*
1840–1841 Visit to England
1843–1844 Visit to England
1848 *Orlandino*
1849 (May 22) Death of Maria Edgeworth

Maria Edgeworth

1
Maria Edgeworth:
From Birth to Death

Maria Edgeworth was born in 1767 (or was it 1768?) and died in 1849. Though born in England, she lived the greater part of her life in Ireland, where her father had spent most of his boyhood. To question whether she was an Irishwoman is to quibble. The family had been in Ireland almost two centuries when she was born; though the English Ascendancy meant that there were two social Irelands, they existed together, inextricably confused, on one small island.

Thomas Lovell Edgeworth, the father, an intelligent Georgian Irish buck, made a hash of things at Trinity College Dublin and went on to Oxford to retrieve his education. But propinquity (Maria makes much of propinquity in her novels) gave him Anna Maria Elers for a wife and Richard for a son before he was twenty. Maria was the third child (the second to live), born two years later. Before the mother died in 1773, there were two more daughters.

Richard Lovell Edgeworth's second marriage, to Honora Sneyd, followed less than four months on the death of Maria's mother. In Honora he found a congenial and capable wife. He had first met her in the civilized society of Lichfield, presided over by Erasmus Darwin, made up of the Cathedral clergy and their wives and children. Here he enjoyed the stimulation of intellect, poetry, scholarship, beauty, and fun. Perhaps he went to France to escape from the temptations of Lichfield, to which he returned, as soon as he was free, to claim his second wife. This marriage would last seven and a half years.

Apparently in Honora were joined most of the virtues, including the capacity to be a responsible mother and teacher to Maria. From Honora too came some of the ideas about children and their education that found their way into the writing that Maria was to do. She was beautiful, and she was competent. Hers were the qualities that characterize many of the impressively handsome and virtuous women that appear in Maria's novels of manners.

With her father and mother Maria paid her first visit to Ireland at the age of six. This visit for Maria lasted upwards of two years and ended when she was sent back to England to school. That is a long time in the life of an intelligent, impressionable child; and though she disclaimed remembering much about it, it may have been long enough in Maria's case to provide the tendency to write the local color that distinguishes her stories and novels that have an Irish setting. It would be at this time, though she may not have been completely happy, that she first knew her father intimately, that she became really aware of his warmth, his liveliness, his attention to business, his curiosity, his contrast with the local Irish character, and his concern for her developing mind and character. The Edgeworths returned to England in 1776, though the father went back to Edgeworthstown in 1779 to tend the decaying estate; and though Maria spent a good part of her time from 1775 to 1802 in boarding school, she was in close touch with her family.

Honora died in April 1780, and on December 25, 1780, Mr. Edgeworth married Honora's sister, Elizabeth Sneyd. In 1782 the whole family returned to Edgeworthstown. From the age of fifteen to the end of her life Maria lived in Ireland.

There is every indication that she had a happy life. Mr. and Mrs. Edgeworth were in love. Maria loved them both. To this third marriage, which lasted seventeen years, nine children were born, so that there were twelve children to be educated by Mr. and Mrs. Edgeworth with the help of Maria.

She had more to do, though, than to educate herself and her brothers and sisters. Mr. Edgeworth was a good proprietor of a big estate and a good businessman. There were leases to be assigned, rents to be collected, lawsuits to conduct, his decisions as local magistrate to be rendered, the house to build up, the land to be improved, politics to be dabbled in, employees to be directed, mechanical experiments to be conducted, entertaining to be done, the ill to be tended, education to be fostered, and the life of a big family to be conducted with joy and responsibility and steady improvement. In what part of these did Maria play

a part? All of them. For she was her father's good
right hand. He shared all his thinking with her and
asked her to participate in all his activities. She was
not permitted to be the detached adolescent, the young
lady of the manor looking on. Without being a pov-
erty-stricken peasant, she came to know the peasant
inside out. But as a member of the gentry she knew
the gentry. She was living to the full the life that she
would write about, and at the same time she and her
father and her stepmother were doing considerable
writing. From 1791 to 1793 the family lived in England,
where Maria made some acquaintance with English
fashionable life.

The third Mrs. Edgeworth died in 1797. On May
31, 1798, Mr. Edgeworth married Frances Beaufort,
younger even than Maria. Mr. Edgeworth described
her as "A young lady of small fortune and large accomplishments,—compared with my age, much youth
(not quite thirty), and more prudence,—some beauty,
more sense,—uncommon talents, more common temper,—liked in my family, loved by me." The first
months of their marriage coincided with the Rebellion.
The two maiden sisters of the second and third wives,
who had come to make their home with the Edgeworths in 1795, elected to stay on. To Frances Edgeworth were born six children, the last in 1812, when
Maria was forty-five years old.

The time to do the major writing by which Maria
won her reputation had now come. She had always
written, but now she was to be a writer. Essays on
education and illustrative stories for children came
first: *Letters for Literary Ladies,* in 1795; *The Parent's*

Assistant, in 1796; and *Practical Education,* of which she wrote a good part, in 1798. *The Parent's Assistant* consisted of stories that illustrated the educational ideas of *Practical Education.* These for the most part have disappeared from the reading of all but the most ardent Edgeworthian.

But in 1800 appeared the novel for which she will always be remembered, *Castle Rackrent.* From that time on she was a writer, an author—successful, self-assured, a woman of the world, though she retained the simplicity and modesty that had marked the first thirty-three years of her life. In 1801 came the publication of her first major novel of manners, *Belinda*; the first volumes of short stories for small children under the general title of *Early Lessons,* but bearing the titles of *Harry and Lucy, Rosamond, Frank,* and *The Little Dog Trusty* in various editions; and the five-volume *Moral Tales,* a sequel to *The Parent's Assistant* made up of short stories for older children. In 1802 came the *Essay on Irish Bulls* by Maria and her father; in 1804, *Popular Tales,* a two-volume collection of stories, one with as many as sixteen chapters, another with eleven; and in 1805 another novel, *The Modern Griselda.*

This is really an impressively large production. For Maria Edgeworth was busy at other things too. There was a visit to England in 1799, when she formed acquaintances with Dr. Darwin, Mrs. Barbauld, and Sir Humphry Davy that were indicative of the company she was to keep all her life. The French Professor Pictet in his account of his visit to Ireland in 1802 speaks of "the celebrated Maria." Mr. Edgeworth was deeply involved in the affairs of the Rebellion and the events leading to the Union of 1800. And of course Maria shared his acquaintance, if only by report, with the leading people of Ireland in these matters.

In 1802 Maria accompanied Mr. and Mrs. Edgeworth to Paris. On the way, in England, they visited slate quarries, copper smelters, and pottery works. This interest in manufactories, coupled with the Edgeworthian interest in scientific experiments and inventions, had considerable influence on the person that Maria was and the writing that she did. It brought her into intimate acquaintance with men of power and business acumen.

The extension of the Edgeworths' acquaintance continued in Belgium, and then in France came familiar association with the Abbé Morellet, de Prony, Berthollet, Montgolfier, Dumont, Mme. Gautier, Mme. Delessert, the Marquis of Lansdowne, Mme. de Pastoret, the Suards, Mme. d'Ouditot (Rousseau's Julie), Mme. Récamier. Was there anyone of importance in Paris that she did not know? All this is important in assaying the authenticity of the pictures of high life that were to come in her novels and shorter tales. More than that, this acquaintance contributed invaluably to her understanding of human nature. It was in Paris also that she received a proposal from a Swedish diplomat and refused him; on the testimony of Mrs. Edgeworth, she loved him.

The Edgeworths returned to Edgeworthstown in 1803, from which time on Maria must have been immoderately busy. She prepared for the press her *Popular Tales*—1,066 pages of fiction in the first edition. She wrote the novel *Leonora* (published in 1806) ; she began *Emilie de Coulanges* (1812) and *Ennui* (1809), both sizable novels; and she wrote *The Modern Griselda* (1805). No doubt she overworked. While she was ill she made her first acquaintance with Scott's writing (*The Lay of the Last Minstrel* in 1805), an experience of no small importance; in 1806, she was much interested in the marriage of her friend Kitty Pakenham to the Duke of Wellington, and in 1808 she first read Madame de Staël. And all the time Edgeworths were dying and marrying and being born, visiting and receiving visitors, being excited by rebellion, worrying about the eldest son, Lovell, interned in France during the war, and—of course—writing. *Emilie de Coulanges* was finished in 1808, and she was working on *Vivian,* another novel of considerable length. Most of her fiction she read aloud to the assembled family.

All this time work was going ahead on *Professional Education,* which was finally made ready in 1808 and appeared in 1809. It bore the name of R. L. Edgeworth, but Maria carried much of the burden of research and writing, as well as the correspondence with experts to whom the chapters were submitted for criticism. She described it as "the object of my waking and sleeping thoughts." The professions with which it deals are those of clergymen, country gentlemen, statesmen, princes, lawyers, soldiers and sailors, and physicians. Anyone acquainted with her fiction will recognize at once the reflection of these interests in the characters that she develops.

Tales of Fashionable Life in two parts and six vol-

umes came out between 1809 and 1812. Miss Edgeworth
had made the first sketch of one of the shorter novels,
Madame de Fleury, as early as 1803, basing it on her
acquaintance with Mme. Pastoret, who had been the
teacher of the royal princess and whose husband had
been teacher of the dauphin and president of the
First Assembly. Besides *Madame de Fleury,* the first
three volumes contained *Almeria, The Dun, Manoeuvring,* and *Ennui.* The last three volumes contained
Vivian, Emilie de Coulanges, and *The Absentee.*

This production alone, without reference to her
earlier writing or what came after, would insure her a
place in the history of English literature. *Ennui, Vivian,*
and *The Absentee* are all large novels. And *The Absentee* is one of the three or four novels that can be
set apart from all her other writing as having a per-
manence of quality and readability beyond anything
else that she wrote.

At this point, 1812, Maria Edgeworth had achieved
more than half of her literary output. She was yet to
do several things superbly well; but her permanent
importance—or lack of it—would not be changed by
what was yet to come. In the field of education her
reputation was international. In Ireland she was a
leading citizen. In England and Scotland she was a
celebrity. Francis Jeffrey wrote in *The Edinburgh Review,*

The writings of Miss Edgeworth exhibit so singular an
union of sober sense and inexhaustible invention, so
minute a knowledge of all that distinguishes manners or
touches on happiness in every condition of human for-

tune, and so just an estimate both of the real sources of enjoyment and of the illusions by which they are so often obstructed, that we should separate her from the ordinary manufacturers of novels and speak of the *Tales* as works of more serious importance than much of the true history and philosophy that comes daily under our observation.

That is a just appraisal today.

And apparently everybody agreed with Jeffrey. On a visit to London in 1813 she was the celebrity of the hour. Everybody sought her out; she knew everybody. Personal acquaintance only strengthened the opinion that people of distinction had formed from her writing.

Apart from her essays and stories for children she had published *Castle Rackrent, Belinda, Vivian, Ennui,* and *The Absentee,* and other fiction that these novels dominate. More was to come.

In 1814, the year when her brother, after eleven years, was released by the French, came *Continuation of Early Lessons,* the stories of *Frank* and *Rosamond* and *Harry and Lucy.* But more important in that year was the vast *Patronage,* a novel that "was too ponderous to be popular and was much criticized." The story had its inception with Mr. Edgeworth in 1787. It was on Maria's mind in 1809, and she was working at it in 1810 (keep in mind all that was to be published by her by 1812).

Between the appearance of *Patronage* and 1820 she issued *Readings on Poetry* (1816) ; two really important novels, *Harrington* and *Ormond* (both in 1817) ; *Comic Dramas*—three three-act plays (1817) ; and her

last major work but one, the *Memoirs of Richard
Lovell Edgeworth, Esq., Begun by Himself and Concluded by His Daughter, Maria Edgeworth.*

For she had come to the watershed of her life in
1817 with the death of her father.

The relationship between Richard Lovell Edgeworth
and his daughter Maria calls for attention. In the
bearing that it had on her writing it has constituted
a vexed problem. It derives in part from his character
and personality, which have only recently found perceptive treatment. In his teens he was a gay blade;
how gay may be judged by his close friendship with
Sir Francis Delaval, a famous Georgian rake. Until
1782, with some interruptions, he was an absentee
landlord. These facts account, certainly, for two major
themes of Maria's fiction. His early interest in education, of which young Maria was one object, was a
major motivating force of his life; Maria caught his
enthusiasm so that their collaboration became so close
that much of their work is indistinguishable. He was
a moralist, and Maria in her writing never surrenders
her moral preoccupation. He became a responsible
landlord and a responsible Irishman; when Maria became the landlord she carried on his enlightened practice, and her political voice became a voice to be
listened to in the land. He was a man of the world,
and she became the friend of the great and the near
great. He was interested in all practical and mechanical
matters, and her writing and management of affairs
reveal a similar preoccupation. Whatever he wished
her to do she wanted to do. He conceived many of
the fictional ideas, such as *The Freeman Family* in the

1780s, that became novels, such as *The Absentee* in 1812. His approval excited her with pleasure; his disapproval was awful to her. People either took to him amazingly well or were repelled by his air of self-sufficiency and self-satisfaction.

As far as Maria was concerned, Richard Lovell Edgeworth could do no wrong. She was convinced that whatever she accomplished was owing to him. Some critics consider his influence on her achievement to be a blight; but, then, the alternative would seem to have been no literary accomplishment at all. If that is the case, we must accept his influence as being for the good.

At any rate, she felt, when her father died in 1817, that her life had come to an end. Because he had charged her with the task of completing his memoirs, which he had taken only to 1782, she devoted herself to it until their publication in 1820. Her brother Lovell became the head of the family presumptive, but more and more, as the years passed, the financial and management burden of the estate and family affairs fell on her, until in 1826 she took full charge. Her stepmother, the two maiden aunts, and various brothers and sisters stayed on at Edgeworthstown.

From 1820 until the appearance of *Helen* in 1834 her only published books were children's books. The goal of illustrating in fiction the moral and practical purposes of the Edgeworthian educational principles was endlessly pursued. She found it congenial because it fulfilled her father's purposes. No doubt before his death he had been acquainted with—or had supplied—many a kernel of the plots. In 1821 came *Rosamond:*

A Sequel to Early Lessons, much of which she wrote
in 1820 while visiting in Paris; in 1822, *Frank: A
Sequel;* in 1825, *Harry and Lucy Concluded.* Under
the title of this last book came these words: "The
business of Education, in respect of Knowledge, is not,
as I think, to perfect a learner in all or any one of the
sciences; but to give his mind that disposition, and
those habits, that may enable him to attain any part
of knowledge he shall stand in need of in the future
course of his life."

In 1817 she published three plays for children, *Little
Plays,* as volume 7 of *The Parent's Assistant.* Her father
had been involved in these at least as far back as 1808.
In 1829 *Garry Owen,* a little story, was printed in
America.

And then, in 1834, came her last major book, *Helen,*
so successful a novel as to sustain fully the reputation
that her earlier novels of manners had won for her.
Her last story, one for children, *Orlandino,* appeared
in 1848.

These bare bones of publications are far from giving
the full story of Maria Edgeworth during these years.
It was not long after her period of desolation following
her father's death and the completion of the *Memoirs*
that she was traveling to England, to France and
Switzerland, to England again, and in 1823 to Scotland.
Everywhere she was the familiar of the famous, the
industrious, the prosperous. She moved from house
to great house meeting politicians, writers, artists, and
actors (Mrs. Siddons), social workers (Mrs. Fry), educators, scientists, and proprietors. She mingled with
"six different and totally independent sets of scientific,

literary, political, travelled, artist, and the fine fashionable, of various shades." Why is it that this prosperous, successful, animated, intelligent woman of the
world is always slipping out of focus, as if her keen
analysis of social problems were an accident, her realis-
tic observations just a happy hit, and her sharply delineated problem novels the mere product of a country
study? Is it because she was so diminutive—little more
than four feet seven inches? She once called herself a
"monster dwarf of an authoress." Or is it that some
one with such a fund of common sense and domestic
virtue cannot impress us as the easy and sought-after
companion of men and women who make the world
go round? But the facts are there to be known and
to be brought to bear in studying her novels.

In 1823 came one of the great events of her life,
becoming acquainted with Sir Walter Scott. He had at-
tributed to her the inspiration to do in his writing about
Scotland what she had achieved for Ireland in her
writing. In their correspondence they came to like
each other. "Sir Walter Scott was always quoting Miss
Edgeworth, or alluding to some of her characters."
They met at Scott's house in Edinburgh. He wrote
then of her: "Miss Edgeworth is at present the great
lioness of Edinburgh, and a very nice lioness. She is
full of fun and spirit; a little, slight figure, very active
in her motions, very good-humored, and full of enthusiasm." A little later she spent two weeks at Abbotsford with the Scotts, a period of time that Lockhart
described as "one of the happiest in Scott's life." Of
Scott Maria said: "Altogether, he was certainly the
most perfectly agreeable and perfectly amiable great

man I ever knew." He was to visit her at Edgeworthstown in 1825. Their friendship was to last until his
death. Of them both Lockhart wrote:

> In Maria he [Scott] hailed a sister spirit; one who, at the
> summit of literary fame, took the same modest, just, and
> let me add, *Christian* view of the relative importance of
> the feelings, the obligations, and the hopes, in which we
> are all equally partakers, and those talents and accom-
> plishments which may seem, to vain and short-sighted
> eyes, sufficient to constitute their possessors into an order
> and species apart from the rest of their kind.

A major adventure awaited Maria in a tour of
Connemara in 1833. Her Irish writing was behind her,
so that her journey through the wilds of western Ireland and her stay at Ballynahinch Castle could con-
tribute nothing to her fiction. But what she found was
confirmation of what she already had created. In 1834
came her last important piece of writing, the novel
Helen, which followed in the tradition of *Belinda* and
Patronage.

Her literary achievements were now at an end.

From 1834 until her death in 1849 there is little
to tell that casts brighter light on Maria Edgeworth the
writer or Maria Edgeworth the novelist. Her brother
Lovell's failure in the management of his school and
of the estate brought the family to the brink of ruin,
from which Maria saved them by buying the estate
all into her own possession. She worked constantly to
help the tenantry. She made visits to England and to
friends in Ireland. She continued to rise above repeated
bereavement. She threw all her energies into aiding

the poor during times of the famine, during one of which (1847) she wrote *Orlandino.* She received distinguished visitors and kept up a voluminous correspondence.

Over a span of fifty years and more someone might speak now and then in slight disparagement of her. Lockhart, not always generous, described her at Abbotsford as "a little, dark, bearded, sharp, withered, active, laughing, talking, impudent, fearless, outspoken, Whiggish, unchristian, good-tempered, kindly, ultra-Irish body." Some reported that she talked too much. What a talker she must have been! Her reading was wide and deep, her perceptions were keen, and her reasoning was sound, so that she really had something to talk about. She laughed heartily; she recognized a joke when she heard it, and she could make one. She loved theatricals. She enjoyed finery and appreciated luxury, but mostly in others; Edgeworthstown was solid and comfortable, but not beautiful. She doted on companionship and did much of her writing in the living room or library, surrounded by that numerous family. She was extremely practical, but generous. She had a good critical sense for the writing of others.

She had the deepest sense of the obligations that her advantages placed her under. Justice guided her father's relations with the tenantry and, after his death, hers too. "A gentleman's estate should be a moral school and the moral education must depend on the justice or kindness with which the proprietor acts." In a country where religious fervor gave fuel to hatred and suspicion she practiced tolerance. She ever deplored party spirit as contributing to the evils of society. All these characteristics and attitudes show forth in her fiction. But her imagination created the shapes of her fiction and informed her style, and the reality of the life she knew provided the stuff out of which she wrote.

2

Writings in the Service of Education

Richard Lovell Edgeworth, with his wife Honora and his third wife, Elizabeth, laid the groundwork for Maria's interest in education. He had made more than one false start before he arrived at the theories that were to be developed in his essays and Maria's stories. But even as he wasted his opportunities for a college education, he was extending his knowledge, classical and philosophical and mechanical. He was much excited by the educational theories of Rousseau and went so far as to rear his first child, Richard, by those theories. But the experiment was so much a failure— Richard was the only one of the children to be poorly educated—that the father, with Honora's help, developed new and more successful ideas that attracted the attention of all Europe. "I claim for my father," Maria wrote, "the merit of having been the first to recommend what Bacon would call the experimental method in education." The Edgeworthian writing on education has been described as the most important since Locke. And anyone who reads it now will be struck by the common sense and the psychological rightness that permeate it.

Every evidence points to the happiness of the Edgeworth family. Learning and happiness went hand in hand at Edgeworthstown House. "We have already," Maria writes, "in speaking of the early care of infants, suggested that the temper should be attended to from the moment of their birth," and "Great care should be taken to prevent occasions for ill-humour. . . ." "By patiently endeavoring to discover the causes of terror in children, we may probably prevent their tempers from acquiring many bad habits." "Every one, who has had any experience in the education of such children as are apt to form strong associations, must be aware, that many of those fits of crying, which appear to arise solely from ill-humour, are occasioned by association . . . : it is, therefore, best to conquer them as soon as possible."

With happiness in mind as both a condition and a goal of good education, what practical ideas are central in the Edgeworths' theories? Proper toys will develop good habits and a sense of industry. "Why should we early disgust children with literature, by the pain and difficulty of their first early lessons?" "To fix the attention of children, or, in other words, to interest them about those subjects to which we wish to apply, must be our first object in the early cultivation of the understanding." Children should be brought to the ability "to reason with precision and to invent with facility." "To children, every mode of instruction must be hurt-

ful which fatigues attention. . . ." "Those who neglect
to cultivate the affections of their pupils, will never
be able to excite them to 'noble ends' by 'noble
means.' " "We cannot foresee on what occasions presence of mind may be wanted, but we may, by education,
give that general command of abstract attention, which
is essential to its exercise in all circumstances." Obedience "must be taught as a habit. By associating pleasure with those things which we first desire children
to do, we should make them necessarily like to obey;
on the contrary, if we begin by ordering them to do
what is difficult and disagreeable to them, they must
dislike obedience." "Oppression and terror necessarily
produce meanness and deceit, in all climates and in
all ages; and wherever fear is the governing motive in
education, we must expect to find in children a pro-
pensity to dissimulation." "The fewer the laws we
make for children, the better . . . ; the letter and the
spirit should both agree. . . ." "With children who have
been reasonably and affectionately educated, scarcely
any punishments are requisite." "Childhood . . . ought
to have as great a share of happiness in it as it can
enjoy compatibly with the other seasons of life . . . ;
by this rule, we may avoid unnecessary severity and
pernicious indulgence."

And so through more than five hundred pages of
Practical Education on the topics that are listed in the
bibliography. It is sententious, yes, but it is clear and
direct. It is reasonable. It is practical. These are characteristics that marked her way of living; these are
characteristics that mark her fiction.

Maria was writing stories before these ideas shaped

themselves into theory. As the educational ideas were being aired in the family library, as she participated in the actual education of her brothers and sisters according to those theories, she was conceiving and writing the stories that exemplified the ideas. In 1791, when Mr. and Mrs. Edgeworth were in England and the children were left behind in Maria's charge, she entertained them by reading the stories that she wrote out on a slate, and having tested them, put them into final form. Her first known story is "The Bracelets"; "The Purple Jar" and "Mademoiselle Panache" are two other early stories.

The beginning of "The Bracelets" quickly establishes the fact that two little girls, Cecilia and Leonora, students in Mrs. Villars's school, are competing for a prize for successful application, compared with which "nothing so much contributed to preserve a spirit of emulation in this little society." Then follows this paragraph:

> Cecilia was of an active, ambitious, enterprising disposition; more eager in the pursuit, than happy in the enjoyment of her wishes. Leonora was of a contented, unaspiring, temperate character; not easily aroused to action, but indefatigable when once excited. Leonora was proud, Cecilia was vain: her vanity made her more dependent upon the approbation of others, and therefore more anxious to please than Leonora; but that very vanity made her, at the same time more apt to offend; in short, Leonora was the most anxious to avoid what was wrong, Cecilia the most ambitious to do what was right. Few of their companions loved, but many were led by Cecilia, for she was often successful; many loved Leonora, but none were ever governed by her, for she was too indolent to govern.

This is nice. Only one of these girls will win the

prize. Actions and incidents determined by character will determine the winner. Here, in her first fiction, we have the pattern for story after story, for many a novel. This fact will come clear in the discussions of the novels. She has a lesson to teach, if we but have the patience and good sense to learn. There is no doubt that she has the capacity to attract attention. Is the reader curious to know who will win the prize?

The teacher of the school in which Leonora and Cecilia are pupils is Mrs. Villars, a pattern of the teacher who cultivates affection, stimulates the desire of emulation, and measures out proper rewards. Here is the first sentence of the story: "In a beautiful and retired part of England lived Mrs. Villars; a lady whose accurate understanding, benevolent heart, and steady temper, peculiarly fitted her for the most difficult, as well as most important of all occupations—the education of youth." In each of her more memorable novels, *Castle Rackrent* excepted (*Castle Rackrent* must always be excepted), there is a person of the type of Mrs. Villars, dignified, wise, and just, who serenely rides above the misgivings and errors of the Cecilias and Leonoras who are involved in the romantic episodes.

In "The Bracelets" Cecilia performs a foolish act, pays a penalty, and comes to the end of the story a wiser child. In "The Purple Jar"—certainly the most popular and best known of her stories—Rosamond acts foolishly, pays a penalty, and becomes a wiser girl. Her mother had determined on a certain amount of money to spend. Faced with the choice of buying the purple jar or a pair of shoes that she needs, Rosamond chooses the pretty jar, which turns out to be filled with colored water!

"Mademoiselle Panache" contrasts a wise and a foolish mother, a sensible young girl and her less-than-sensible sister, the two well-taught sisters and a girl who has a foolish French governess. As a result of the frivolous and irresponsible teaching of the governess, her pupil develops habits of folly and dishonesty.

Dishonesty is frequently either the main concern or a secondary problem in these stories. In "The False Key" an honest servant boy of thirteen, well brought up, protects his mistress from the thievery of a dishonest serving boy and the drunken butler. In "The Birth-day Present" a spoiled, petulant little girl's dishonesty is contrasted with the stubborn honesty of another child.

In "Lazy Lawrence" the boy who will not work steals, after losing at gambling, from the boy who, by initiative and hard work, manages to get enough money together to save his widowed mother's horse from being sold for rent money. Often the theme of honest industry is woven in with the ideas of a commonsensical or foolish education and dishonesty or honesty. Of course the honest child, whose instruction has been sound, thrives. In "The Little Merchants" an irresponsible Italian father teaches his son dishonesty, while a wise father rears his son always to be honest. Virtue pays. In "The Basket Woman" some honest children are inadvertently paid for some service by a guinea instead of half a crown; when they go to much trouble to find the absent-minded man, he rewards them with a blanket for their grandmother and lessons in basket making by which they can earn a living.

The ideas, as fiction, are ingenuous. And the style, fittingly, though embroidered, is ingenuous. "The Basket Woman" opens with these sentences: "At the foot of a steep, slippery white hill, near Dunstable in Bedfordshire, called Chalk Hill, there is a hut, or rather a hovel, which travellers could scarce suppose to be inhabited, if they did not see the smoke rising from its peaked roof. An old woman lived in this hovel, and with her a little boy and girl, the children of a beggar, who died and left these orphans perishing with hunger. . . ." "The Orphans" begins: "Near the ruins of the castle of Rossmore, in Ireland, is a small cabin, in which there once lived a widow, and her four children." This is a pretty exactness, not too detailed or precise, that invites the reader to make a picture for himself, to make a moving picture in the imagination, perhaps, to accommodate the action of the characters.

"The Barring Out" and "Simple Susan" tend to invite a somewhat weightier appraisal than the other stories. The author's imagination in these is more striking because more unusual. The type of complication anticipates the complications that animate the novels that she was to write later. The two central characters of "The Barring Out" are teen-age boys in Doctor Middleton's boarding school. The headmaster is a wise, tolerant, fair man. But a new boy, Archer, fired by ambition and supported by confidence in his abilities, leads the other pupils to lock themselves in a common room to force the headmaster to capitulate to their demands. A sit-in! Opposed to Archer is De-Grey, up to this time the generous leader of a contented student body. Maria may have developed the story from fact (and she often did so), for the ingenious devices and episodes have the ring of truth. The wise doctor, in the end, reinstates all the boys except one, named Fisher, who is expelled because he has been guilty of real baseness.

There is much weak, or even wicked, human nature in the stories. "Were young people," Maria (or her father) writes in the preface to *The Parent's Assistant,* ". . . absolutely free from bad examples, it would not be advisable to introduce despicable and vicious characters in books intended for their improvement. But in real life they *must* see vice, and it is best that they should be early shocked with the representation of what they are to avoid. There is a great deal of difference between innocence and ignorance."

Shocked, yes, and intrigued. Sermonizing was probably no less uncongenial to children in the 1790s than it is today. But something about this sermonizing made it better than merely acceptable, and it may well be this quality of psychological realism that becomes evident time and again. Just as the goody-goody quality tends to pall, the clear-eyed realism counteracts it.

The accusation has been made that "we read her shallow stories and swallow her specific for happiness as a hypochondriac might swallow quack medicine—not because it seems so easy and infallible." This judgment is open to question. The moral issues are reduced to a kind of ultimate simplicity, yes, but "simple" is a more nearly accurate word than "shallow."

The stories have that quality which in painting is called "primitive," a word that we can accept precisely because of the type of picture that it describes. We must add to that judgment, however, our awareness that Maria Edgeworth had a trained intellect and a steadily widening experience. In the 1790s, and until that time, she was learning her craft.

The stories about Rosamond and Frank that she wrote later (she was still writing them in the 1820s) lost the primitive quality as she gained the experience of controlling long plots, of devising varieties of incidents, and of manipulating psychology with greater subtlety. *Frank: A Sequel to Frank in Early Lessons* runs to 241 pages in the 1825 American collected edition. That is a long, long story, through which Frank is taken from the age of seven to the age of ten or eleven. *Harry and Lucy* is altogether over a hundred pages. And *Rosamond* through four parts and the *Sequel to Rosamond,* spanning perhaps thirty years in the writing, extend to 245 pages. Certainly the earlier stories, those written in the late 1700s, were a testing ground for the novels; but the novels provided the experience that gives persuasiveness to the later stories.

It would be vain, probably, to suppose that Frank and Harry and Rosamond could command a reading public today. Frank's father takes pains to teach Frank, at seven, the method of making beer. And then there is wine:

> After dinner Tom was at his mamma's elbow "for his glass of wine." This day it was to be a bumper because there was company.
> "True, my dear, because you must drink all the com-

pany's health, and master Frank's in particular."

"Oh, mamma, that's not a fair bumper yet," said Tom.

"Well, now my dear, there's a fair bumper for you—quite a man's bumper.—I will treat you like a man and gentleman today, because, Tom, you were very good today, in not swinging on my Chinese gate, which is the only thing, you know, I forbid.—Aye, you remember! You lost your wine once by that—Oh, I am very strict, ma'am sometimes: pray give me credit. But, Tom, how you tossed it down, without recollecting all the healths—I'm quite ashamed."

Tom, with his head back as far as it could be thrown, was in spite of his mother's shame, trying if a drop more could not be had from the bottom of the glass.

His mother observed, "that it was very odd Tom had learned to like wine so, for she could remember the time when he could not bear the taste of it. But, my dear master Frank, you must get your bumper too—Mamma will allow you a bumper this once—today, I am sure."

But mamma will not allow Frank his bumper this once—she has much too much sense for that. Tom's purpose in the story is to show all the weakness of character and habit that Frank's parents, by educating him well, enable him to avoid.

There is a circumstantiality in the passage about the wine that has the ring of truth, although the scene is totally foreign to us. This power of circumstantiality shines out time and time again as Frank's education continues apace. He learns how to thatch, to make bricks and to build with them; he learns ancient history and Latin grammar; he masters a horse but rejects the temptation to be a hunter; he has his flirtation with gambling; he studies the heavens; he conquers his vanity; he develops courage and endures pain; he puts up with taunting, accepts disappointment, and refuses to flatter.

This is all by way of preparing him to go away to public school, where the less than perfect teaching and control of the boys will make such virtues as he has attained stand him in good stead. Miss Edgeworth was a realist and a utilitarian (her father looked to Bentham with veneration). Success and happiness were the parents' goal for Frank, and she gives parents practical instruction in getting a boy ready for the education that was then available. "Every father, every mother," she says, "can by preparatory care, direct the home education of their boys before they send them to school."

The girls are not neglected. Frank has a girl companion, who takes the place of the sister and exemplifies, in all she does, the education that is appropriate to a girl. This is the purpose of Rosamond, of course, who has to suffer the pains of her own shortcomings as she progresses through innumerable adventures from the unhappy choice of the purple jar to the moment when she makes the sensible choice of an excellent horse, when she is in her teens.

Certainly the problems of Rosamond's character and that of Frank have the ring of truth—and often the excitement even now of interest. "Action should be introduced—Action!—Action!" Mr. Edgeworth wrote concerning stories for children. "Whether in morals or science, the thing to be taught should seem to arise from the circumstances, in which the little persons of the drama are placed; and on the proper manner, in which this is managed, will depend the excellence and success of initiatory books for children." Many of the incidents, surely, derive from the family life of the Edgeworths: "The first part of Harry and Lucy was written by me [RLE] thirty-four years before Frank and Rosamond were written by my daughter," and Honora Edgeworth was keeping a record of daily experiences with children in the 1770s. The badinage of brother and sister particularly has the ring of give-and-take within the family.

The last volumes in this extensive writing on education were *Harry and Lucy Concluded; Being the Last Part of Early Lessons,* issued in 1825. They continue the education of Harry and Lucy largely in science. The first lessons are in the principles of the barometer, the hygrometer, and the air pump. Maria is still using *The Botanic Garden* (1791) of Dr. Darwin, her father's great friend, for illustrations. When the uncle of the children gives them his own hygrometer, he says, "I give it to you in the hope that it will teach you accuracy and patience," and they keep a daily record of its readings for half a year. Throughout, Maria is careful to differentiate between the two children. Lucy is much too quick and inattentive; her mind jumps around. But Harry is too comprehensive and driving. Lucy quotes poetry, and Harry, who is fascinated by scientific problems, learns some liking for poetry from her.

In the Preface to *Harry and Lucy Concluded,* Maria writes:

Harry and Lucy was begun by my father, above fifty

years ago, for the use of his own family, and published at a time when no one of any literary character, excepting Dr. Watts and Mrs. Barbauld, had ever condescended to write for children. That little book was, I believe, the very first attempt to give any correct elementary knowledge or taste for science in a narrative suited to the comprehension of children and calculated to amuse and interest, as well as to instruct. Finding, from experience, that it answered the intended purpose, my father continued the book at intervals; and in the last part, published in 1813, I had the pleasure of assisting him. . . .

I have endeavored to pursue, in this *Conclusion of Early Lessons,* my father's object in their commencement —to exercise the powers of attention, observation, reasoning, and invention, rather than to teach any one science, or to make any advance beyond first principles. The essential point is to excite a thirst for knowledge, without which it is in vain to pour the full tide even to the lips.

And further:

All attempts to cheat children, by the false promise, that they can obtain knowledge without labour, are vain and hurtful. The gods sell every thing to labour, and mortals, young or old, must pay that price.

No better comprehensive statement about the purposes and methods of the Edgeworthian writings can be made. There remains only to demur at her curious pretense, at that late date, that almost all the work was her father's and that it was only toward 1813 that she gave assistance in the writing on education.

3

Some Moral Fiction

Between 1801 and 1812 Maria Edgeworth published twenty-two volumes of fiction. Among all these titles are six major novels of extended length and complication and at least three other major works that can be designated novels. Published during this same period were *Early Lessons, Essays on Professional Education,* and *Essay on Irish Bulls.* Up to this point there has been only passing mention of her greatest and most enduring fiction, *Castle Rackrent,* published in 1800.

These publications represent a most impressive productivity. She produced all this while writing, more often than not, in the library at Edgeworthstown, surrounded by father, aunts, stepmother, innumerable brothers and sisters, and a steady stream of visitors. What is remarkable is not that some of these stories are not particularly successful, but that a great number of them are, still, eminently readable. We begin to understand how she could deserve the epithet, in comparison with Sir Walter Scott some years later, the Great Known.

Of all these titles *Belinda* and *The Absentee* stand out as two major novels that deserve extended attention. Two others somewhat in the same category are *Ennui* and *Vivian*. These four novels will be treated in other chapters. Of those titles that remain *Forester, The Modern Griselda, Leonora, Madame de Fleury,* and *Emilie de Coulanges* probably call for the most attention.

Why the word "tale"? Maria makes a point of calling *Belinda* "A Moral Tale." The first edition of *The Modern Griselda* labels it a tale. For Maria the word was significant. She wrote in a letter, "Though I am as fond of novels as you can be I am afraid they act on the constitution of the mind as drams do on that of the body."

Not wishing to acknowledge a novel, Maria wrote:

> Were all novels like those of Madame de Crousaz, Mrs. Inchbald, or Dr. Moore, I would adopt the name of novel with delight. But so much folly, errour and vice are disseminated in books classed under this denomination, that it is hoped the wish to assume another title will be attributed to feelings that are laudable, and not fastidious.

The impulse to teach asserts itself so that, with the word "moral" appended to most of these stories, we can expect to find ourselves instructed and edified.

Criticism of the novel as a literary form is scattered throughout all her fiction. She differentiates always between popular love romance and the tales of terror, on the one hand, and novels of purpose, on the other. The following passage appears in "The Good French Governess":

In their way home, Mad. de Rosier stopped the carriage at a circulating library. "Are you going to ask for the novel we were talking of yesterday?" cried Matilda.

"A novel!" said Isabella, contempuously: "no, I dare say Mad. de Rosier is not a novel-reader."

"Zeluco, sir, if you please," said Mad. de Rosier. "You see, Isabella, notwithstanding the danger of forfeiting your good opinion, I have dared to ask for a novel."

"Well, I always understood, I am sure," replied Isabella, disdainfully, "that none but trifling, silly people were novel-readers."

"Were readers of trifling, silly novels, perhaps you mean," answered Mad. de Rosier, with temper; "but I flatter myself you will not find Zeluco either trifling or silly."

"No, not Zeluco, to be sure," said Isabella, recollecting herself; "for now I remember Mr. Gibbon, the great historian, mentions Zeluco in one of his letters; he says it is the best philosophical romance of the age. I particularly remember *that,* because somebody had been talking of Zeluco the very day I was reading that letter; and I asked my governess to get it for me, but she said it was a novel—however, Mr. Gibbon calls it a philosophical romance."

"The name," said Mad. de Rosier, "will not make such difference to *us*; but I agree with you in thinking, that as people who cannot judge for themselves are apt to be misled by names, it would be advantageous to invent some new name for philosophical novels, that they may be no longer contraband goods—that they may not be confounded with the trifling, silly productions, for which you have so just a disdain."

Richard Lovell Edgeworth, despite his frequent officiousness, comments justly on the *Moral Tales* in his introduction. "These Tales have been written to illustrate the opinions delivered in 'Practical Education' "—and no little of the pleasure in reading them, for the person who is acquainted with *Practical Education,* derives from the recognition of principles of Edgeworthian education in their fictional form. Forester in the tale named for him is an eccentric nineteen-year-old who refuses to conform to the common usage of society —neatness, mannerliness, consideration for the privileges of his elders; but the unhappy results of his unconventionality bring him to a reasonable conformity, so that he can even participate in the frivolity of dancing because it gives general pleasure. In "Angelina, or L'Amie Inconnue" Maria ridicules the nonsense of sentimentality and romantic eccentricity. " 'Mademoiselle Panache' is a sketch of the necessary consequences of imprudently trusting the happiness of a daughter to the care" of a frivolous and unprincipled governess; while Mademoiselle de Rosier in "The Good Governess" illustrates in fiction the appropriate techniques for teaching children. The Good Aunt manages by prudence to rear her nephew well, in contrast to boys whose character is ruined by silly parents and bad tutors.

Except in *Mademoiselle Panache* there is no concern with romance whatever; but except for this lack of love interest these stories adumbrate the interests and concerns of the major novels that begin with *Belinda*.

How organized, how disciplined Maria is, how clear and settled her purpose, begins to be plain when one examines all the writing being considered here. Naturally, from 1795 until 1812 there is not an uninterrupted progression; but a reasonable, orderly, and intellectual progression there is. *Castle Rackrent* is the major interruption—1800. *Belinda* is another—1801. Then *The Modern Griselda*—1804 and *Leonora*—1806.

With the *Tales of Fashionable Life* she is bringing her great work in education to its logical conclusion by illustrating the effects of education on young adults in *Almeria, Madame de Fleury, The Dun, Manoeuvring,* and *Emilie de Coulanges.* At the same time she is writing the full-fledged romances or novels *Ennui* and *Vivian;* and in 1812 she caps the climax with *The Absentee,* a mature, fully extended, highly imaginative novel beyond which she is not destined to go.

There is a flutter of romance in *Forester* and *Mademoiselle Panache* as early as 1801. She will have been observing the teen-age crushes, the first flirtings with love, the first marriages among her cousins and brothers and sisters. *Belinda* deals very much with the problems of love affairs, but breaks down on motivation and improbabilities of circumstances. Courtship and marriage supply the impetus to action in some of the *Popular Tales.* In *Vivian* the complications of love are more interesting and at the same time more frustrating. And then comes the maturity of *The Absentee,* which has been in incubation many and many a year and which, in the interrelationships of social conditions and personality involvements, works a love affair through all possible let and hindrance to a happy marriage.

The Modern Griselda and *Leonora* are two serious studies of marriage. What are the characteristics of the good, the successful wife? Maria Edgeworth's answers are plain, for she is always careful to make evident the lessons that she is teaching; but in these instances certain shortcomings inhibit the liveliness and persuasiveness of her points.

In *Leonora* the woman of virtue is contrasted with

Olivia, whose lack of principle and self-understanding leads her to betray Leonora's trust and take Leonora's husband away from her. In the end Leonora's excess of virtue wins the man back. But in the modern point of view he would hardly be worth having, for the psychology of the main characters is not acceptable, though the problem that Maria sets is a sound one, worthy of exploration. The epistolary technique becomes a kind of straitjacket on both action and analysis.

The problem of *Griselda* is a real one too—the wife who refuses to be contented and pushes a good husband beyond the power of enduring her unreasonableness. The heroine forfeits all sympathy, for her unreasonableness is more stupid than wrongheaded. Maria does better stories of marriage than this elsewhere.

The stories of *Popular Tales* are all of generous length, from forty to ninety pages, having the character as well as the length of the short novel and being kept within the dimensions of a stated problem pursued along a fairly straight line to a solution. Each illustrates certain virtues that the young person not so fortunate as to be a nobleman or a clergyman or a gentleman might do well to cultivate. It is in this aspect that the stories are called "popular"—that is, there are fewer readers among the nobility, clergy, and gentry than there are among the common people.

In *Lame Jervis* Miss Edgeworth makes the point that a young man will serve himself best by being honest and industrious and by learning to read and write. In *The Will* young John Wright (note the name) wins the legacy over Grimes Goodenough (who will not try anything new) and Pierce Marvel (who puts all his faith and effort into harebrained schemes). In *Out of Debt Out of Danger* the young man loses through foolishness the fortune that his father had amassed by industry and thrift.

Etcetera—that word will suffice for the *Popular Tales*. Still, they have a kind of ingenuous charm. More important than their inherent characteristics, though, is the practice that they provided for the novelist who was yet to write *Patronage*, and *The Absentee, Ormond,* and *Helen*.

4
Two Novels of Manners:
Belinda *and* Helen

Whether Maria called *Belinda* (1801) a moral tale
or not, it was her first full-dress, full-blown novel about
love and manners. Thirty-three years later came her
last, *Helen* (1834). There is little to choose between
them. They are contained within the same limits of
plot, character, and setting. In between she pushed out
those limits in some other novels: *Patronage* is noteworthy for its great length and complication; *The Absentee* is noteworthy for its exemplification of a major
social problem; *Ormond* stands out for its unusual
success with a hero and the fascination of its setting;
Harrington may have been the first novel to bring the
question of discrimination against Jews into focus.

But *Belinda* (*Castle Rackrent* is always excepted)
defines her talents. Indeed, it sets her pattern, to which
almost all her fiction thereafter conforms, and to which
her last novel provides almost an exact match. Among
the novels of her day it set a high standard, and many

a time thereafter she performed up to that standard and on some occasions exceeded it. *Belinda* deserves examination.

Belinda starts off with an admirable first chapter. There is no doubt that here is a novelist in full control of formidable talents. She seizes the reader by his lapel, and with a self-confidence that approaches virtuosity she sets out quickly the basic stuff of her story. There is a scheming, social-climbing Mrs. Stanhope, who has the last of six nieces yet to marry off (we meet Mrs. Stanhope only through her revealing letters). The niece is Belinda, eighteen, accomplished, mannerly, intelligent, attractive. Belinda is spending the winter in London with Lady Delacour, fashionable, brilliant, witty, dissipated. Lady Delacour's husband, a viscount, is drunken, jealous, debauched, and alienated from his wife. A constant companion of Lady Delacour's is a youth in his twenties, a late-eighteenth-century rake, Clarence Hervey, who is attracted to Belinda and attractive to her. Within a few pages the essential tensions are established. Within the next few pages that make up the second chapter the complications are well under way, most of the characters are introduced, and the train of circumstances is set rolling down its long track at exciting speed.

Chapter II. Clarence is unlikely as a prospective husband because a niece of Mrs. Stanhope is thought to be a trap. Lady Delacour is dying from cancer of the breast.

Chapters III and IV. Lady Delacour's history—an unhappy marriage; two dead children and a third who is not allowed to remain at home; death by a duel and a duel between women; wild extravagance, dissipation, and enmity.

Chapters V, VI, VII. Lady Delacour's shamelessness and dissembling about money frustrate Clarence's growing attraction to Belinda. He endangers his life in rakish living, but in being saved comes under the influence of the noble Dr. X—— and the Percivals. "What a pity, Mr. Hervey, that a young man of your talents and acquirements, a man who might be anything, should—pardon the expression—choose to be a nothing."

Chapters X and XI. Lady Delacour is injured in a carriage accident, Lord Delacour exhibits the remains of affection. It is hinted that she may not have cancer. Sir Philip Baddely and Mr. Rochfort, two foppish rakes, discover that Clarence is keeping a mistress.

And so through thirty-one chapters until Clarence and Belinda are married, Lord and Lady Delacour are restored to marital felicity and have their daughter Helena with them, Lady Delacour is saved from death, the supposed mistress finds a true lover, and all Belinda's world is distinguished by virtue and happiness.

There is a sorry amount of absurdity scattered through all this, and perhaps we should look at the absurdity first. The supposed mistress of Clarence is Virginia St. Pierre, a girl in her teens being reared by Clarence to be his wife. This situation is less absurd for Maria than it is for her readers, for Mr. Edgeworth's great and good friend Thomas Day had once taken two young girls to rear with the intention of making one of them his wife. Mr. Edgeworth had been involved in the undertaking, which must have been a subject of much discussion at Edgeworthstown. But the absurd in true love is not convincing enough for fiction, and if *Belinda* founders it founders on the story of Clarence's mistress.

But how much that is good remains! The story of Lady Delacour's cancer is truly affecting. Where in fiction has such a problem appeared before? The subject is shockingly real; the psychology of the treatment is often deeply penetrating; the cause and ramifications of the cause are novelistically ingenious. Indeed, the entire creation of Lady Delacour is a major achievement. "Lady Delacour was governed by pride, by sentiment, by whim, by enthusiasm, by passion—by anything but reason." She is a fashionable beauty, past her prime, frustrated in marriage and motherhood, challenged in her pride by all the fashionable goings-on and competitions of high society. There are all the trappings of dress and servants and smart horses and carriages; of balls and morning visits and gallery showings; of servants and tradesmen and royalty and noblemen. In the artificiality of such a life she fights a duel, of all things, and is injured on her breast by the recoil of her gun.

For all the fancifulness of this incident, we seem to be seeing an authentic picture of high life in the time of George III. The women duelers dressed in men's garb bring Caroline Lamb to mind. Maria knew about such things. She knew the qualities of happy domestic life; and it is likely that, even if she did not observe much strife between husband and wife, she could infer what such strife is like. Lady Delacour so hates her husband that she will not run the risk of receiving his pity by letting him know about her cancer. In her headstrong pride and frustration she is ready to submit herself to the knife in the hands of a quack, after aggravating the wound through agonizing months with worthless medicines.

Lady Delacour has been marked by many a critic, but Lord Delacour has waited a long while for the acknowledgement that he deserves. He is not in the spotlight so much as she, but when he is on stage he holds his own. We see him first, dead drunk, being carried upstairs by his servants. For a while we can understand Lady Delacour's repulsion. Together they exemplify the evils of marriage for money, title, and position. But woven into the love story of Belinda and Clarence is the reconciliation of the Delacours, tentative, gradual, psychologically motivated. When Lord Delacour's pity is stirred by his wife's cancer, when his daughter is returned home, when he is convinced of his wife's fidelity—gradually as the pieces are fitted into the reconstructed marriage—he redirects his life toward respectability.

Maria's success with the young buck is always impressive. Clarence is acting like a fashionable irresponsible young fool when we first meet him and is risking his life in an irresponsible, drunken shenanigan when the circumstances begin that lead to his rehabilitation. His companions are two fashionable young men of the town, Sir Philip Baddely, who cannot open his mouth without swearing, and Mr. Rochfort, stupid in action, dress, and principle. Their feminine counterparts, who come close to being the villains of the novel, are Mrs. Freke, whose country house is called Rantipole, and Mrs. Luttridge, who runs a gambling salon.

The point of significance here is the comprehensive range of Maria's power of character creation from the despicable to the ideal (where always she is weakest). For a woman whose severe morality is always deprecated she shows a surprising knowledge of the world and an impressive breadth of understanding; even acceptance. In *Belinda* appear the first of her interesting servants, Lady Delacour's maid; the first of her termagant but virtuous old ladies, Lord Delacour's aunt; the dishonest manservant Champfort; the devious and self-serving old lady, Belinda's Aunt Stanhope; and an elderly lady of the world, Lady Boucher. To balance these are characters virtuous beyond all bounds, and therefore out of the bounds of interest, but their presence does not obliterate the presence of those characters that are faulty in principle or manner or understanding.

Of course the counterparts of all, good and bad, have been scattered through her stories, as have the childhood figures that grow into her heroes and heroines in her novels of manners. And in her last novel of manners, *Helen,* they are all present again.

Helen, the impecunious orphan, is virtuous beyond reproach. Might her name not be Belinda just as well? She lives with General Clarendon and his wife, Lady Cecilia Clarendon, of impeccable social standing and immense wealth; they correspond to Lord and Lady Delacour. She is courted by Beauclerc, young, immensely wealthy, headstrong. But just as Hervey's supposed mistress is an impediment to marriage to Belinda, so the fact that Beauclerc is "as good as married" keeps Helen from looking forward to being his wife. In time of trouble with the friends with whom she is living, Belinda takes refuge with the virtuous Lady Anne Percival; in trouble likewise Helen takes refuge with the virtuous Miss Clarendon, sister to the General. Lady Cecilia's mother, Lady Davenant, in whom Helen confides, has the social brilliance of Lady Delacour and the virtuous wisdom of Lady Anne Percival. Lord Delacour's servant Champfort is a villain inimicable to Belinda's welfare; Lady Davenant's servant Carlos threatens Helen's welfare. Belinda is courted by the unprincipled fop Sir Philip Baddely; Helen is courted by the unprincipled fop Horace Churchill. Belinda knows two unprincipled women, Harriott Freke and "the odious Mrs. Luttredge"; Helen knows two un-principled women, Lady Louisa and Lady Katrine. And in the end the impediments to true love are removed, and a happy future lies before both couples.

Such a presentation seems to argue against the novelis-tic achievement of the author. Has she no more imagi-nation than to tell the same story twice? Such a question can be misleading. There is no argument about the fact that the two plot lines are parallel. If the novels are both in large part successful, the success must derive, then, from elements other than the complica-tions of the stories. Let us make it our business to know what those elements are.

Is it possible that the very characteristic for which Maria has been blamed, her moralism, is a major source of interest in both novels? Yes, it is. The reader today

will find that his interest derives largely from the lesson
that she means to teach. The lesson takes its definition
from the characters and their interplay. The tensions
among the characters derive from the moral weaknesses
that they show.

Certainly the most interesting character of *Belinda*
is Lady Delacour. She is not a good woman; she may
even be sinful. Her supposed cancer derives from her
irresponsibility and willfulness. She is extravagant beyond all reason. She is a failure as a wife, she is a failure
as a mother. She is intemperate in manner and action,
sometimes beyond the point of foolhardiness. Such a
woman is a threat to the innocence of a younger woman
put in her charge.

Belinda by herself is hardly interesting, but Belinda
threatened does make an appeal, and the threats to her
welfare and innocence provide the commentary on
society that Maria wants to make. The innocent young
Helen, just entering the world, likewise is threatened;
and we are interested, not in her goodness, which is
pallid enough, but in the psychological penalties that
she pays for compromising truth to protect her friend in
the friend's dishonesty.

Helen is a novel about truth and lying. Lady Cecilia's
falsehood is akin to Lady Delacour's cancer and as
deadly. One lie leads to another, until Cecilia's marriage and Helen's prospects of married happiness are
all but destroyed. How Maria brings about a happy
ending is little to the point. The interest lies in following the deterioration of character and the penalties
that both the guilty and the innocent have to pay.

The moral issues shape up in some splendid dra-

matic scenes. The headstrong Beauclerc's first clash
of wills with his guardian, General Clarendon, is taut
with temper and the coruscating clash of disparate
personalities. Each scene in which the waspish, fashionable bachelor, Horace Churchill, plays a part strips
the veils away from the shallow pretensions of smart
society; but beyond that, he takes upon himself gradually the lineaments of a feeling human being even
as his meanness and pettiness and female venom become
more and more pronounced. This is comedy of manners
at its best, fit for the stage. There is a scene in the
dentist's office that is absolutely from the life. We wish
that Helen would speak up and defend herself; that
someone would give Cecilia a crack and straighten her
out; that Lady Davenant would be less sententious. But
the long delay of resolution gives time for suspense to
build. Will innocence reveal itself? Will truth prevail?
Will youthfulness give way to mature good sense? Will
rigid self-righteousness bend? Maria sets a valid problem and, with sentimental lapses now and then, provides a valid solution. Such without sentimentality
would seem to be the stuff of successful fiction.

Some of Maria's less successful novels should be
noted. Besides *The Modern Griselda* and *Leonora,*
which we have already glanced at, there are *Manoeuvring, Almeria, Madame de Fleury,* and probably *Emilie de Coulanges* in *Tales of Fashionable Life.*

Everywhere in them are evidences of the essential
Edgeworth: a lesson to teach, a right psychology, a
sharp sense of scene, telling conversation. But what
she does well here she does better elsewhere, and our
time might be better spent with the really good things.

In these she usually drives too straight toward her
mark. In *The Modern Griselda* a happy marriage
quickly deteriorates into failure because the wife insists
on dominating her admirable husband. There is little
suspense to delay the deterioration. *Leonora* deals with
the essential contrast between right sensibility in the
wife and wrong sensibility in the temptress. It is a
story of adultery and the return of the wandering husband to his patient wife. The mistress "has a sort of
morbid sensibility, which is more alive to pain than
pleasure, more susceptible of jealousy than of love."
Penetration into character becomes inextricably confused with absurdities of plot. Maria is always tolerant
of the double standard, but her tolerance of the mis-
behaving husband goes beyond all reasonable bounds.

The lesser novels of *Tales of Fashionable Life* are the
stories of *Moral Tales* and *Popular Tales* matured and
developed. The shortest is *The Dun,* twenty-six pages;
but in that space a family is brought close to starvation
by a callous coxcomb, the daughter of the family is
lured to the brink of prostitution to save her loved
ones, the coxcomb draws back from forcing the girl
to be his mistress and is reformed. The social problems
to which it points are worthy of a scope much bigger
than the summary treatment that they receive here,
and they do sting awake the moral conscience of the
reader: Dickens would follow in the train of novels
like this one.

Almeria and *Madame de Fleury* travel pretty much
the straight track from starting point to destination.
Almeria climbs the social ladder with her fortune,
forgets her early friends, and ends an embittered, card-

playing old maid. Madame de Fleury, because of kindness to some poor children and the sensible education that she gives them, is saved from the French Revolution and eventually restored to her estates. The events of *Manoeuvring* are concerned with matters less threatening than starvation and death and revolution; but the conflicts, which derive from essential qualities of human nature, develop into a scintillating novel of manners. A mother who maneuvers to marry her son and daughter off so as to gain for them fortunes and titles is tricked by her own tricks, while her children find happiness by remaining true to themselves. There are plenty of lessons here, too, but Miss Edgeworth succeeds in creating idiosyncratic characters whose qualities are convincing, so that the conflicts between characters take on urgency and suspense.

Something of these qualities appears in *Emilie de Coulanges*. The romance is little more than silly, but the woman who does good and resents the recipients of it, the French woman who cannot give up her integrity even to be saved from destitution, and Emilie, who is caught in between, are products of true imagination and skill.

5

Castle Rackrent (1800)

Early in her career Miss Edgeworth wrote her greatest novel. It was something entirely new, for it treated the Irish character, aristocrat and peasant, with absolute authenticity and integrity. It has the value of the coin newly minted out of the pure ore. It has the richness of economy possible only to the well endowed. It mines veins not before explored. It set an example followed by some of the world's great novelists. And it stands all alone, for she never wrote another story like it.

No harm can be done by retelling the story.

Thady Quirk tells the story in the first person. He is steward to the Rackrents, whom his family have served for generations, but who have run out their line. The Rackrent properties now belong to Thady's son Jason.

The first of the Rackrent line was Sir Patrick, who spent his money riotously and drank himself to death.

The next owner was Sir Murtagh. He married a woman named Skinflint. Between them they bled the peasants white, but he lost much of the property in lawsuits and died of a stroke in the midst of a fight with his wife, who departed with a rich fortune.

Sir Murtagh's successor was a young officer, Sir Kit, who lived a life of profligacy as an absentee, turned over his accounts to Jason, married a Jew for her money (which he did not get), bamboozled the ladies, and got himself killed in a duel.

And now we come to Sir Condy, the young heir-at-law. We have had, up to now, a fine overture. The main body of the composition here begins.

Sir Condy's character has room for all the shortcomings of his forebears save parsimony. Added to his weaknesses is a modicum of weak-minded endearingness. He learned to drink as a child, when he started to become dependent on his playmate Jason. He fails to put his college and law education to good use, borrows against his expectations of coming into the estate, starts going into debt to Jason, sells away or forfeits his land in parcels, chiefly to Jason; makes an unfortunate marriage in expectation of money, but the wife turns out to be as profligate as he; goes more deeply into debt and drinks heavily and entertains more wildly; loses an immense sum in running for office; is deserted by his wife; signs everything over to Jason; and dies while taking a deep draught of whiskey.

The whole novel takes up little more than sixty pages. Why is such a slight story a major achievement in the history of English fiction?

The answer lies in the subject matter, the characterization, the local color, the wit and irony, the style, the plot, the humor, and the tragedy. It is all the stuff of greatness, wrapped in the subtlety that comes from total control. Its success derives, too, from the absence of certain tastelessness in plot, lapses of style, repetitiveness of incident and character. *Castle Rackrent* is the first of its kind, ingenious, imaginative. It is quite impossible to think of another novel since that outpaces it on its own ground. Certainly Maria never wrote anything else to enter into competition with it. Scott says that he went to school to it, and there is evidence that Turgenev did too; undoubtedly Thackeray was influenced by it. And whoever has gone to school to Scott and Turgenev and Thackeray derives, to some degree, from *Castle Rackrent*.

The subject matter has already started to come plain. Maria in her preface calls this a tale of other times. She says that "the race of Rackrents has long since been extinct in Ireland; and the drunken Sir Patrick, the litigious Sir Murtagh, the fighting Sir Kit, and the slovenly Sir Condy, are characters which could no more be met with at present in Ireland, than Squire Western or Parson Trulliber in England." We can take her at her word if, in the 1790s, there was neither drunkenness nor litigiousness nor fighting nor slovenliness in Ireland. And if we should take her at her word, we should be quite as wrong as if we took the surface tale of *Castle Rackrent* to be the real tale that she is telling. But more of that point later.

The story that she tells is that of successive generations of the Rackrent family who have lost their all and their lives through their weaknesses which, one may suppose, they share with many of their Irish fellows. As they forfeit their property, bit by bit, an unscrupulous, avaricious peasant gets it into his own hands, until at the end the Rackrents are no more, and one who has been a propertyless servant now holds title to everything.

All that is interesting enough, but the characterization is deep and exact and dismayingly perceptive. The character of each man, each woman, is made naked. Among them all there is no wisdom, common sense, forbearance, generosity, kindness, clear-sightedness, or even common decency. The Rackrents are damned. And Thady, his son Jason, and his niece Judy are damned too. No Rackrent is exactly as Thady the narrator depicts. Nor are Jason and Judy. Nor is Thady the man that he depicts himself to be.

Only the truly serious mind could make such humorous judgment on the tragic frailties of mankind. The texture is thick with exact observation of character, speech, detail of dress, or farming practice or custom. The first Rackrent is too improvident to put a gate on his fence and is killed when he tries to take his horse over the cart that fills the gap. Sir Murtagh's wife "had a charity school for poor children, where they were taught to read and write gratis, and where they were kept well to spinning gratis for my lady in return"; and she bled the tenants of their fowl and pigs and horses as bribes for their leases, while her husband cheated them into starvation in his way. As a boy Sir Condy would stop at the cottages "to drink a glass of whiskey out of an eggshell [eggshells would be there, though a drinking glass were not], to do him good and warm his heart, and drive the cold out of his stomach," and early became a drunkard. Details like this make up the riches of this story.

And the irony, which peeks out of these short quotations—how like a dissecting knife it is. The most ironic word of all throughout the novel is the word "faithful"—"faithful Thady," the steward, who tells this tale in the first person when he is beyond his eightieth year. So skillful is Maria that the quick and careless reader may finish the story without detecting the guile with which Thady had managed to turn his employer's weaknesses to his own advantage. Every word of praise is actually a perceptive revelation of the Rackrents' errors and the Quirks' avid quickness at taking advantage of them. The Rackrents play always into Thady's and Jason's hands, though, if a reader were inattentive, he might think exactly the opposite. One could weep at this tragedy of barefaced human nature; one must laugh at the mischievous perceptivity that turns it all to humor.

6
Three Tales of Fashionable Life: Ennui, Vivian, The Absentee

Ennui (1809—written in 1804), *Vivian* (1812—written in 1809), and *The Absentee* (1812), appeared, along with five other tales, under the general heading of *Tales of Fashionable Life.* Their heroes might well be the boys of *Harry and Lucy* and *Frank* writ large. Their heroines might be—let's see, who *are* the heroines of these stories? Miss Edgeworth's purpose to instruct is as strong as ever, and in them she sets about her purpose of teaching lessons with the imagination, humor, and dedication that mark all her fiction. *Ennui* is a relative failure—its story tends to grow murky in the memory. *Vivian* is a relative success—it has some characters and develops some tensions that mark some new achievements in fiction. *The Absentee* is good altogether—it is a major novel.

One cannot get past the miserable fact that the plot

of *Ennui* hinges on the hero's being a changeling. The Earl of Glenthorn is not the Earl after all, but the real son of the old Irish nurse Ellinor. And when the truth is known, the false Earl and the true Earl resume their natural places, to the total destruction of a family that had been happy peasants and the regeneration of the man who had been losing his soul, through ennui, as the Earl. In the end he even gains back the estate by marriage to the girl who has been waiting in the wings since the early pages of the book. Such stuff adds up to a total handicap much too severe for the novel to recover from. The fact to be remarked is how much Miss Edgeworth manages to accomplish under such a handicap.

Much of the strength of her fiction derives from her powers in conversation and in the creation of scene. Too little of these powers is evident here. The success of the first-person telling of *Castle Rackrent*, with the ironical revelation of the narrator's peasant cupidity, does not insure a similar success in the first-person telling by a rich young man of fashion. What in *Castle Rackrent* is inherent in story and character is, in *Ennui*, a surface layer, like varnish. The Irish scenes have the ring of truth, like the marvelous progress of the Earl and his servants from Dublin to his castle at the mercy of Irish horses and Irish drivers. Even the castle, wildly romantic, is convincing to one who knows the Connemara coast. The servants, the castle hangers-on, the poor blacksmith-turned-earl all fit the scenes and the situations like the real people that they are and might well have contributed to the growing involvement of the novel, in the British Isles and on the

Continent, with the common man. Like the peasants, the scenes of the 1798 insurrectionists derived from Miss Edgeworth's very real experience. But the story moves ahead in patches. The hero's evolution from wastrel to successful lawyer is hardly convincing, and the romance serves no other purpose than plot.

If *Ennui* reveals the evils of lassitude, *Vivian* reveals the evils of indecision, of indecisiveness. "My son," R. L. Edgeworth's mother had once said to him, "learn early how to say No!" He must have told the story often, and Maria must have been much impressed. In *Vivian* she drives the lesson home.

By being infirm of purpose (a French edition bears the title *Vivian, ou l'Homme Sans Caractère*), Vivian moves from riches, promise, love, and ambition in the first scenes to shame, failure, unhappy marriage, and death at the end. Much of this is truly convincing, perhaps because in this novel Miss Edgeworth is not burdened with the necessity of bringing about a happy ending. (Of the major novels, in *Castle Rackrent* and *Vivian* only do the protagonists come to a bad end.) Her hero, then, lacks the dimensions of the conventional hero of romance; he is truly a weakling. The heroine is as forgettable as almost all her heroines, virtue unadulterated; but the wife that Vivian ultimately takes, Lady Sarah Glistonbury, is an original. At first view she is repellent to the reader and to Vivian alike. As Vivian becomes entangled morally, financially, and politically, the fear that he will be caught in marriage by Lady Sarah gradually grows. But in the end, if he is to have redemption, that redemption can come only from her. Neither he nor she is saved, by which

time the worth of both is so well established that their
defeat has the quality of tragedy.

One other character, were his matrix a novel more
successful than *Vivian* is, could take his place among
the notable characters of early-nineteenth-century fiction. It is Lord Glistonbury, Lady Sarah's father—an
unwise, unprincipled, powerful politician, whose ma-
neuverings to maintain political power and to gain a
marquisate catch Vivian up in a net of wrongdoing
that ends in destruction.

A word about style. However many the good things
of character and incident, they can hardly survive a
style that can be represented truly in an example of
a few short words: ". . . continued she, in a tone of
proud humility." There is too much of that kind of
artificiality, that archness, that false elegance, which in
their dead weight submerge a host of good things.

The Absentee was a good novel in 1812 and is a
good novel today. Its wellspring was a problem of
great social importance: the absentee landowner whose
cupidity and indifference to the tenants' welfare
brought suffering to the peasantry and tragic deterioration to government. For social Ireland of Miss Edgeworth's time there was no subject of deeper concern.
She laid it out plainly and powerfully for the absentees
to see their own shortcomings and the sad effects of
those shortcomings.

A good subject is not enough. What can the novelist
do with it? Can he create a world in which the subject
is the moving force, populate it with people for whom
the reader feels concern, and manipulate the action
through the requisite tensions to a reasonable resolu-

tion? In *The Absentee* Miss Edgeworth does all that. Her father had experienced absentee ownership. When he returned to Ireland to reclaim the management of his estate himself, she participated in all the experiences every foot of the way, always with the estates under absentee ownership evident for observation and comparison. She knew well the Anglo-Irish of the Establishment, the fashionable Englishman, and the Irish peasant. She had had long experience in fashioning plots.

Some of the shortcomings of the fashionable novel of manners are here. The heroine, Grace Nugent, is an orphan of questionable ancestry who, in time to be an eligible bride for the hero, turns out to be a legitimate child and an heiress to boot. The hero is too virtuous and too competent for a twenty-one-year-old. The Bradys, who represent the dispossessed peasants, are somewhat too genteel. The reader should indulge himself in some indifference to these so that he can relish the successes of the novel in full measure.

Like the shortcomings, the successes are largely in the characters. Lady Clonbrony hardly deserves sympathy, selfish, stubborn, social-climbing wife and mother that she is; but she gets it, for she is not happy in the delusion of being fashionable and must find happiness in returning to Ireland and her responsibilities there. Lord Clonbrony should have put his foot down years before, but we like him the more for suffering under the selfish domineering of his wife. Sir Terence O'Fay epitomizes the Irish characteristics of wit and improvidence and shrewdness and impertinence. The excellent Miss Broadhurst has the blunt good sense and downright asseveration of the Miss Clarendon of *Helen*. The wicked agent Garraghty and the exemplary agent Mr. Burke enliven the contrast between good and bad estate management. Individualistic secondary characters, as usual, abound. The triumph of the good characters is long delayed and is realized only after threats and ruses and risks and dashes, so that the long tale races on in a thoroughly pleasant, lively fashion.

And through all, the lessons get themselves thoroughly taught. Ireland would be a much better nation if only the landowners would stay in Ireland and tend to their business. Happiness and well-being attend good sense and virtue; prosperity attends good management. Toadyism gets paid off in bad currency. The lessons are lessons that Ireland needed. It would have been much better off if the Irish—aristocrat and peasant, merchant and politician, old and young—had sat attentively to Miss Edgeworth's teaching.

The happiness of the Edgeworth family in one another's company, the prosperity of the Edgeworth estate, their service to the tenantry and the poor, their contribution to husbandry, government, education, and practical comfort—all these attest to the warm good sense and wisdom from which the author derived the attitudes that she dressed in such a tale of imagination as *The Absentee*.

7
Three Major Novels: Patronage, Harrington, Ormond

These major novels are, in length, approximately 313,000; 104,000; and 139,000 words. That is a prodigious (Miss Edgeworth calls that a feminine word) amount of work. Each has excellences that make it stand out from her works. And all three have just about been forgotten. Our fictional resources would be richer if they could be restored to the reading canon.

Patronage was at least twenty-six years in the writing —not continuously, of course. Mr. Edgeworth was telling the story in the family circle as early as 1787, and each day his daughter wrote down what she had heard. In 1809 she began seriously to shape the novel, which gave her a great deal of trouble. The material that became the novel *The Absentee* (1812) was a part of the original scheme and by the route of being made into a play, was extracted and shaped into a separate novel to fill out *Tales of Fashionable Life*.

Each of the four novels was motivated by a purpose different from the purposes of the others. She used *The Absentee* to show the evils of absentee ownership in Ireland, a historical phenomenon. Her purpose in *Patronage* was to contrast the weakening effects of relying on the help of others with the advantages of self-reliance. In *Harrington* she undertook to make amends for the unfavorable treatment of Jews in fiction by writing a story sympathetic with the Jews. In *Ormond* she described the education and character development of a young man. Remembering that *Castle Rackrent* is entirely different from any of these, we must admire the versatility and variety of the author.

Miss Edgeworth always contrasts virtue with vice, strength with weakness, nobility with meanness. These are the contrasts of her early stories, written to educate children and to illustrate her educational principles. In each of her novels these contrasts determine the skeleton on which the body of the stories is shaped. In *Patronage* she manipulates the contrasts with the amazing skill of the virtuoso, weaving pattern into pattern, extending the scope over a vast dramatis personae of more than sixty men and women, concocting a convoluted puzzle that, in the end, resolves itself with the utmost reasonableness in exactly those rewards and punishments that are appropriate to the recipients.

Occasionally vice is too black, virtue too crystalline; such constitute the weaknesses of all her novels. Here it is, probably, that she misses greatness. But to forfeit the whole because Sir Robert is conventionally wicked and Mrs. Hungerford is appallingly good is to deprive ourselves of something that we ought not to do without. *Patronage* ought not to be forgotten. As one takes an admirable human being for what he is worth, shortcomings and all, one should take *Patronage*.

The novel pits two families against each other—the Percys, who are the heroes and the heroines, and the Falconers. In each family there are a father and a mother, three sons, and two daughters. The Percys are self-reliant. They believe in education, diligence, and virtue; and even when their welfare is threatened, they rely on themselves to endure, if not to overcome. The Falconers believe in the main chance, the shortcut, the compromise, and above all in the favors of the powerful. They seem to prosper, with appointments to place and power; but because they are inadequately prepared and are always ready to sacrifice principle to profit, they all fall from grace and sink to a place lower than the station from which they began. The Percys, on the other hand, make their way against threat and setback by remaining self-reliant and honorable, with happy marriages and professional success and wealth their rewards.

The characters of *Patronage* are worth a long and careful study. They display a Dickensian differentiation; their physiognomies, if they were made to represent truly the minds and personalities, would in a group portrait display a striking variety. Each of some twenty minor characters would happily bear the marks of caricature. Mr. and Mrs. Percy, their daughter Caroline, and her husband Count Altenberg would hardly, in their perfection, lure the eye to pause; Sir Robert and Lawyer Sharpe, in their perfect villainy, are mere stereotypes. But to become thoroughly familiar with the others is to enjoy a revel of acquaintanceship.

Two characters of somewhat secondary importance, though representative of types, are each a singular achievement. Lord Oldborough (note the name) is a great political figure who dedicates himself to serving king and country while sacrificing as little of principle as possible; Lady Jane Granville's good heart is always at war with the demands and pretensions of fashionable society. Lord Oldborough's character and actions illustrate the contentions of right and wrong; Lady Jane's illustrate the conflicts between social silliness and family loyalty. Together they blanket professional and social life with the moral instruction that determines the ambience of all Miss Edgeworth's fiction.

A third character, who deserves to hold a place among the strongly delineated characters of fiction, is Buckhurst Falconer. Buckhurst, though self-indulgent as a young man, has enough attributes to be considered as a possible suitor for the perfect Caroline Percy. But his weak nature, inadequate education, and need for income fall in with his father's machinations in favor of his children's preferment, and he comes to the unhappy end of a hateful marriage and the loss of prospects and pride.

Essentially the chief interest of *Patronage* derives from its characters. But Miss Edgeworth contrived a wealth of incident in which the characters act: shipwreck and fire, felony and trial, forfeited property, impressment of sailors, forged wills, and so on and on, with the usual, and less interesting, tribulations of young love. There is a happy issue out of all the afflictions, of course, for those characters who have shown strength of character, and appropriate punishment for all the Falconer faction, who had put their reliance on patronage rather than industry and virtue.

For its attributes *Patronage* provides a profitable reading experience still, though its shortcomings in the way of sentimentality, particularly in its elements of romance, help explain the lack of favor from which it has long suffered.

Harrington and *Ormond* were issued together in three volumes. Because Mr. Edgeworth was seriously ill—he died in June 1817—Miss Edgeworth found it almost impossible to approach the writing of *Harrington,* finished in November, 1816, and then *Ormond,* which her father ordered her to undertake. His displeasure with her lack of industry forced her to carry the two novels to completion.

In *Harrington* she attempted to make amends for the ungenerous treatment of Jews in her earlier fiction. The overt purpose imposes a heavy weight of restraint upon *Harrington,* from which its attributes narrowly fail to rescue it. For the time in which it was written it is a singularly interesting novel. And though for readers of the late twentieth century it sags somewhat, it deals generously and intelligently with a problem that is still moot.

The word *problem* is correct here. It identifies the central issue of the novel, which offers essentially no interest in character. Its plot is certainly of minor importance. But the problem of the place of the Jew in society is a permanently perplexing concern. It was a matter of major dimensions at the time that Miss

Edgeworth wrote, for the question of civil liberties for Jews—their emancipation—was much on the English conscience and mind during the first half of the nineteenth century.

She has received less than appropriate credit for an achievement in *Harrington* that she accomplished only to a lesser degree in other novels: a sharpened psychological study that would do credit to a twentieth-century analyst in fiction. Having established at the beginning of the novel a small child's aversion to Jews and his reasonable fear of them, she then subtly, gradually traces his progress through doubt, reexamination, avowal of the Jew's rights and virtues, to his offer of marriage, against all family opposition, to the daughter of a Jew.

This is no mean feat. When before had this been done in fiction? How soon or how often after 1817 will it be done again?

Harrington's father, a bigoted, well-to-do member of Parliament shows the traditional dislike of Jews and opposition to them. As a little boy, Harrington's nurse, whenever Harrington gives her trouble, threatens him with punishment by an old-clothes-man Jew. All the members of the Harrington circle, all his friends at school, all his associates as a young man, despise and mistreat the Jews. But he draws his own conclusions from what he sees, identifies the psychological source of his own aversions, judges according to the facts, and comes to a just appraisal of his fellow human beings.

The attributes of the novel have suffered inattention because of the weak solution to the romantic problem of having the daughter of the Jew turn out to have a

Christian mother. Miss Edgeworth herself acknowl-
edges that she should have done better than that; she
calls it "an Irish blunder." As in almost all her novels
of manners, she contrives a happy ending for the characters that interest us most, after duels and threats of
loss of fortune, after all kinds of complications of
romance, after opposition and capitulations. But her
achievement still stands—original, humane, and strik-
ingly perceptive.

Ormond is not a problem novel like *Harrington.* It
is not a novel of manners like *Helen* and *Belinda,*
though it shares some of their characteristics. It is not
a mere object lesson like the short stories. It is not an
Irish novel like *Castle Rackrent,* though its chief action
takes place in settings that are distinctively Irish. Of
Ormond Mr. Edgeworth wrote, "The moral of this tale
does not immediately appear, for the author has taken
peculiar care that it should not obtrude itself upon
the reader." We have here some of the reasons that
(*Castle Rackrent* excepted) *Ormond* is Miss Edgeworth's best novel.

Above all *Ormond* is a novel of character, and the
chief character is Ormond himself, a brawling, drinking, half ignorant eighteen-year-old Tom Jones when
we first meet him, a responsible, self-disciplined, fairly
well cultivated young man, quite worthy of the paragon
of all the womanly virtues whom he will marry when
the novel ends. It is Miss Edgeworth's problem to
create the challenges and the solutions through which
Ormond must travel to make the transition.

Two other major characters make the strongest appeal to the reader. Cornelius O'Shane rules the Black

Islands, where much of the most interesting action takes place, like a king; indeed, he is called King Corny. He exemplifies all the old Irish virtues, but mingled with them are all the old Irish shortcomings. Even with all his weaknesses, including drinking, improvidence, and bullheadedness, he is a thoroughly admirable man. Contrasted to him is his cousin Ulick O'Shane, a political manipulator, a toady to the Anglo-Irish and the English, in his character reminiscent of the Falconers in *Patronage,* in birth and education and personality worthy, in action the victim of his weaknesses of character.

Sir Ulick is the guardian of the orphan Ormond. And after Ormond almost kills a man in a drunken anger, Sir Ulick maneuvers him to the Black Islands, where he becomes Prince to King Corny. The contrast between the two households is one of the major strengths of the novel. Most particularly do the Irish characters and customs associated with King Corny have the appeal of the unusual and authentic.

As always, Miss Edgeworth peoples the novel with secondary characters who have the charm of idiosyncrasy: White Connal and Black Connal, twins who, in turn, become suitors for Corny's daughter, Dora, because of a drunken promise made by Corny years before, thus eliminating the more deserving but fortuneless Ormond from entering competition.

In short, Ormond does come into a fortune, resists the temptations of the Court of Versailles, where Dora and her husband run a gambling salon, returns to England in time to save his fortune from Sir Ulick's machinations, and wins both the right girl and the Black Islands for his own.

This is a romance of realism, morals, and manners. It is the work of a wise and authentic story-teller, flawed now and then by conventionality or sentimentality or contrivance, but in the main distinguished by invention, pace, color, the persuasion of verisimilitude, and the excitement of originality.

8

A Summary Appraisal

Richard Lovell Edgeworth died in 1817, very shortly after the completion of *Ormond* and before *Ormond* and *Harrington* appeared in print. He had had much to do with the writing of both novels. Yet to come from Maria's pen were the completion of his memoirs (1820) ; fiction for children and young people in the service of education—*Rosamond: A Sequel to Early Lessons* (1821), *Frank: A Sequel to Frank in Early Lessons* (1822), *Harry and Lucy Concluded* (1825) ; *Little Plays* (1827), three dramas for children; *Garry Owen*, which first appeared in 1829, and *Poor Bob* (1832), two stories for children issued together in a book; the three-volume novel *Helen* (1834) ; and *Orlandino* (1848), a moral tale for young people. Of all this work, only *Helen* contributes importantly to the measure of her reputation. Her father's death was a turning point.

The exact truth about the relationship between father and daughter is elusive. She elevated him above all other human beings in her admiration—"that wonderful father of mine." She deferred to him in all things. She took inspiration from him for her subject matter, wrote some things on assignment by him, collaborated with him, subjected almost all that she wrote to his criticism, admitted some of his writing into her own work, relied on him for business arrangements with publishers, traveled in his train to the social centers of Dublin, London, and Paris, and took into her mental and social, political and artistic self all his standards and strictures.

He could be severe with her. He apparently could hold her coldly at arm's length in his affections when she failed to measure up to his expectations in self-discipline. He put a very high rating on her talent, and only productivity after a period of inertia or self-indulgence in emotion could win him back from pointed disapprobation to affection and support.

His failing health threatened her entire happiness. She wrote to Mrs. Barbauld: "I say as little as I can upon this subject: it is too near to my heart." Two years before his death she was writing: "The spring of his mind has not recovered. He says that nothing excites him, that he feels no motive. This is so unlike him. And it is so very uncommon to see him sad and silent, and utterly passive that it is impossible to resist the contagion." But just as he found the moral strength to rally his spirits weakened by pain and failing in sight, so he expected her to discipline her emotions and harness her talents in full productivity. His death in June 1817 was devastating for her; for some months she was almost incapacitated by the effects of grief. But her father had left her a job to do, the completion

of his memoirs. It was unthinkable that she should
fail him.

"The spring of his mind," she wrote, an apt expression; for his intellect was from his young manhood
wound tight, and produced with strength and regu-
larity and exhilaration a half century of useful work.
All this had a marked bearing on Maria Edgeworth the
novelist. Mr. Edgeworth was something of an engineer,
able to conceive the damming and rerouting of a
major river, to design and build roads, to drain bogs
and put them into agricultural production, to invent
wagons and springs, to design and build buildings and
a multitude of gadgets. He was the owner and manager
of a large estate, and he organized and directed for
many decades a numerous tenantry. He was a local
magistrate and a member of parliament. He managed
a large fortune. He was an educational philosopher
with the practical acumen to put his ideas into practice
and to disseminate them. He was an author. He was the
familiar of the great and the prominent—scientists,
philosophers, manufacturers, statesmen, educators, noblemen.

In all this Maria shared familiarly from childhood.
Surely her writing was shaped in great part by the
disciplined life in which she was an active participant,
a partner. And surely it was discipline, both imposed
and self-imposed, that bound the numerous family
together and enabled them to rise above their tribulations and to meet their challenges.

A summary of the Edgeworthian sorrows may enable
us to do greater justice to Maria Edgeworth than has
ever been done before. First, Maria was six years old

when she lost her mother. She was thirteen when she lost her first stepmother, Honora, and thirty when she lost her second stepmother, Elizabeth. Though she remembered little of her own mother, she revered Honora and loved Elizabeth dearly, so that the death of each was a sore bereavement. Of her brothers and sisters, six died before she was thirty-three. Ten more brothers and sisters died between 1800 and 1849. Two of her brothers had to be confined to a sanatorium because of mental illness.

Twenty deaths of parents and brothers and sisters whom she loved dearly; two situations of mental breakdown by brothers for whom she had the greatest affection; the mental and physical deterioration of another brother, the head of the family after her father's death, whose financial ineptitude brought the family to the edge of financial ruin—this is the stuff of family and personal tragedy. It is impossible to imagine a family through whom the streams of affection flowed more purely and deeply. (Domestic happiness she describes as "the only happiness in this world that lasts.") But such was the self-discipline of Maria, such the resilience of spirit and mind, that after each devastating event she rallied her forces, including her talent of fiction writing, and regained the generosity and the gusto of life that distinguished her into her eighty-second year.

The fiction that she wrote grew from the warmest sensitivity of affection; the rich experience in emotion of all the major events in the life of man; an acquaintance among the most vital men and women of her day; a sharp awareness of poverty and riches; a political and social philosophy sharpened by observation, study, and firsthand experience. She went through a long apprenticeship in writing from early childhood, matured under the firm guidance of her knowledgeable family, and took instruction and inspiration from some of the best authors of her day.

The result was wisdom. Under the burden of her losses she might reasonably have turned to tragedy. But the burden of all she wrote lies on affirmation. Her educational theory derives from a sensitive respect for the capacity and potentiality of the individual; the child was of the greatest importance in her philosophy. She extended this respect to what may be expressed as the more childlike part of society, the uneducated peasantry, and promoted among them the practical virtues of industry, honesty, and self-respect. The simpler virtues she extended into the firmly held ethical principles that provide, either in their observation or abrogation, the patterns of her plots and dramatis personae. She found congenial the orderly construction of her stories and novels that conformed to the orderly disposition of her ethics. To intellectuality she joined humor and fun, industry and application, inquiry and analysis, discernment and good sense.

Her initiative came from the wellspring of imagination; thus, she wrote *Castle Rackrent* and set loose the movement of local color. The treatment of the peasant in his own setting was absolutely new. She moved on from Richardson and Fielding to develop the novel of manners and gave it a finish that, if justice were done, would renew life in some of her novels for today's readers. She brought honor to Ireland.

Yeats wrote, "The one serious novelist coming from the upper classes in Ireland, and the most finished and famous produced by any class there, is undoubtedly Miss Edgeworth." Scott called her "one of the wonders of our age" and wrote late in his life in the General Preface to the 1829 edition of the Waverley novels:

Without being so presumptuous as to hope to emulate the rich humor, pathetic tenderness, and admirable tact, which pervade the works of my accomplished friend, I felt that something might be attempted for my own country of the same kind with that which Miss Edgeworth so fortunately achieved for Ireland—something which might introduce her natives to those of the sister kingdom in a more favorable light than they had been placed hitherto, and tend to produce sympathy for their virtues, and indulgence for their foibles.

In *The Quarterly Review* a writer remarked that "by the mid-nineteenth century Scott, Maria Edgeworth, and Jane Austen, coming on top of the eighteenth-century quartette, had given the novel the unchallenged predominance in which Dickens and Thackeray confirmed it, and which persists to the present day [1848]."

Yeats and Scott and *The Quarterly Review* do Maria Edgeworth justice.

Selected Bibliography

I. WORKS OF MARIA EDGEWORTH

1. *Tales and Novels of Maria Edgeworth*. The Longford Edition. London, 1893. 10 vols. There are numerous collected *Tales and Novels*. The Longford Edition, the most readily available, can stand for them all. It has been most recently issued in the AMS Reprint Series, 1967; and by Georg Olms Verlagsbuchhandlung (Hildesheim), 1969. Its contents are as follows:

Volume I.	*Moral Tales: (Forester, The Prussian Vase, The Good Aunt, Angelina: or, L'Amie Inconnue, The Good French Governess, Mademoiselle Panache, The Knapsack)*
Volume II.	*Popular Tales: (Lame Jervas, The Will, The Limerick Gloves, Out of Debt Out of Danger, The Lottery, Rosanna, Murad the Unlucky, The Manufacturers, The Contrast, The Grateful Negro, Tomorrow)*
Volume III.	*Belinda*
Volume IV.	*Castle Rackrent, Essay on Irish Bulls,* "An Essay on the Noble Science of Self-Justification," *Tales of Fashionable Life: (Ennui, or, Memoirs of the Earl of Glenthorn; The Dun)*

Volume V.   *Tales of Fashionable Life: (Manoeuvring, Almeria, Vivian)*

Volume VI.   *Tales of Fashionable Life: (The Absentee, Madame de Fleury, Emilie de Coulanges)*
The Modern Griselda

Volume VII. *Patronage*

Volume VIII. *Patronage* (concluded)
Comic Dramas: (Love and Law; The Rose, Thistle, and Shamrock; The Two Guardians [in the first edition])
Leonora
Letter from a Gentleman to His Friend, upon the Birth of a Daughter; Answer to the Preceding Letter; Letters of Julia and Caroline (these three titles constituting *Letters for Literary Ladies*)

Volume IX.   *Harrington, Thoughts on Bores, Ormond*

Volume X.   *Helen*

2. Other collected editions:

a. *Tales and Miscellaneous Pieces.* London: R. Hunter *et al.,* 1825. This is the first collected edition. 14 vols. "It contains all of her writings to that date with the exception of the children's stories and the *Memoirs* of Richard Lovell Edgeworth."

b. *Tales and Novels.* Second Collected Edition. London: Baldwin and Craddock *et al.,* 1832–1833.

c. *Tales and Novels of Maria Edgeworth.* London: George Routledge and Sons [1875].

3. *The Parent's Assistant; or Stories for Children.* London: J. Johnson, 1800. 3d ed. 6 vols. (1st ed. 1796, 3 vols.)

Volume I.   "Lazy Lawrence," "Tarlton," "The False Key"

Volume II.   "The Birth-day Present," "Simple Susan" (not in the first edition)

Volume III.   "The Bracelets," "The Little Merchants" (not in the first edition)

Volume IV. "Old Poz," "The Mimic," "Mademoiselle Panache"

Volume V. "The Basket-Woman," "The White Pigeon" (not in the first edition), "The Orphans" (not in the first edition), "Waste Not, Want Not," "Forgive and Forget"

Volume VI. "The Barring Out," "Eton Montem" (neither in the first edition); "The Little Dog Trusty," "The Orange Man," "The Purple Jar" (last three not in the third edition)

Volume VII. Not published until 1827. *Little Plays:* ("The Grinding Organ," "Dumb Andy," "The Dame School Holiday")

4. *Practical Education.* London: J. Johnson, 1801. 2d ed. 3 vols. (1st ed. 1798, 2 vols.) : "Toys," "Tasks" (largely by RLE), "On Attention," "Servants," "Acquaintance," "On Temper," "On Obedience," "On Truth," "On Rewards and Punishments," "On Sympathy and Sensibility," "On Vanity, Pride and Ambition," "Books," "On Grammar, and Classical Literature" (by RLE), "On Geography and Chronology" (by RLE), "On Arithmetick" (by RLE), "Geometry" (by RLE), "On Mechanicks" (by RLE), "Chemistry," "On Public and Private Education," "On Female Accomplishments, Masters, and Governesses," "Memory and Invention," "Taste and Imagination," "Wit and Judgment," "Prudence and Economy."

5. *A Rational Primer.* By the authors of *Practical Education.* London: J. Johnson, 1799. Developed, with Maria's help, by RLE from a 1780 volume by him and Mrs. Edgeworth.

6. The volumes and editions bearing *Early Lessons* as the title or as part of the title are many. This method of listing may be helpful:

a. *Early Lessons.* 6 vols. London: J. Johnson, 1801. *Harry and Lucy* Part I

Harry and Lucy Part II

Rosamond Part I: ("The Purple Jar" [a repeat], "The Two Plums," "The Day of Misfortunes")

Rosamond Part II: ("Rivuletta" [by her sister Honora?], "The Thorn," "The Hyacinths")

Rosamond Part III: ("The Story of the Rabbit")

Frank Part I

Frank Part II

Frank Part III

Frank Part IV

The Little Dog Trusty: ("The Little Dog Trusty" [a repeat], "The Orange Man" [a repeat], "The Cherry Orchard")

b. *Continuation of Early Lessons.* 2 vols. London: J. Johnson, 1814: ("Frank," "Rosamond. The Wager," "The Party of Pleasure," "The Black Bonnet," "The India Cabinet," "The Silver Cup," "Rosamond. The Bee and the Cow," "The Happy Party," "Wonders," "The Microscope," "To Parents," "Harry and Lucy")

c. *Rosamond: A Sequel to Early Lessons.* 2 vols. London: R. Hunter, 1821. It contains twelve stories.

d. *Frank: A Sequel to Frank in Early Lessons.* 3 vols. London: R. Hunter, 1822.

e. *Harry and Lucy Concluded; Being the Last Part of Early Lessons.* 4 vols. London: R. Hunter, 1825.

7. *Readings on Poetry.* London: R. Hunter, 1816.

8. *Memoirs of Richard Lovell Edgeworth, Esq., Begun by Himself and Concluded by His Daughter, Maria Edgeworth.* 2 vols. London: R. Hunter, 1820.

3d ed. 1 vol. London: R. Bentley, 1844. Revisions made by Maria Edgeworth.

Latest printing (with Introduction by Desmond Clarke) Shannon: Irish University Press, 1970.

9. *Garry Owen; or, The Snow Woman.* Salem: John M. and W. and S. B. Ives, 1829.

Both Mr. Sadleir and Mrs. Slade apparently were unaware of this separate edition. They date the first separate edition as that of John Murray, 1832.

10. *Orlandino*. Edinburgh: William and Robert Chambers, 1848. In Chambers's Library for Young People.
11. Fugitive pieces, found usually in collections:
    a. Notes and Preface to Mary Leadbeater, *Cottage Dialogues Among the Irish Peasants*. London: J. Johnson, 1811.
    b. "The Mental Thermometer" in *The Juvenile Library*. London: T. Hurst, 1801.
    c. "Little Dominick" in *Wild Roses; or Cottage Tales*. London: printed by T. Marden for Ann Lemoine and J. Roe, 1807.
    d. "The Freed Negro," a poem, in *La Belle Assemblée*. London, 1822.
    e. "Thoughts on Bores," an essay, in *Janus; or the Edinburgh Almanack*. Edinburgh: Oliver and Boyd, 1826.
    f. "On French Oaths," an essay, in *The Amulet; or Christian and Literary Remembrancer*. London: W. Baynes and Son, 1827.
12. *Tour in Connemara and the Martins of Ballinahinch*. Edited by Harold Edgeworth Butler. London: Constable and Company, 1950.

II.   BIBLIOGRAPHIES

1. *The Cambridge Bibliography of English Literature*. Edited by T. W. Bateson. Cambridge: University Press, 1940.
2. Slade, Bertha Coolidge. *Maria Edgeworth: A Biographical Tribute*. London: Constable, 1937. An indispensable guide to the earlier editions.
3. Sadleir, Michael. *XIX Century Fiction, a Bibliographical Record Based on His Own Collection*. Vol. 1. London: Constable and Company, 1951. One of the bases from which Mrs. Slade worked.

III. BOOKS OF BIOGRAPHY AND LETTERS

1. Barry, F. W. *Maria Edgeworth: Chosen Letters.* London: Jonathan Cope, 1931.
2. Butler, Harold Edgeworth and Butler, Jessie Harriet. *The Black Book of Edgeworthstown and Other Edgeworth Memories 1585–1817.* London: Faber and Gwyer, 1927.
3. Clarke, Isabel C. *Maria Edgeworth: Her Family and Friends.* London: Hutchinson and Co., 1950.
4. Butler, Marilyn. *Maria Edgeworth: A Literary Biography.* Oxford: Clarendon Press, 1972.
5. Clarke, Desmond. *The Ingenious Mr. Edgeworth.* London: Oldbourne, 1965.
6. *Dictionary of National Biography.* Edited by Leslie Stephen and Sidney Lee. Vol. 6. London: Smith, Elder, and Co., 1908–1909.
7. Hare, Augustus J. C. *The Life and Letters of Maria Edgeworth.* 2 vols. Boston: Houghton Mifflin and Co., 1895.
8. Hill, Constance. *Maria Edgeworth and Her Circle in the Days of Buonaparte and Bourbon.* London: John Lane, 1910.
9. Inglis-Jones, Elisabeth. *The Great Maria.* London: Faber and Faber, 1959.
10. Lawless, Emily. *Maria Edgeworth.* London: Macmillan and Co., 1904.
11. *Maria Edgeworth: Letters from England 1813–1844.* Edited by Christina Colvin. Oxford: Clarendon Press, 1971.
12. *A Memoir of Maria Edgeworth, with a Selection from Her Letters by the Late Mrs. Edgeworth.* 3 vols. Edited by Her Children. London: 1867. Not published.
13. Oliver, Grace A. *A Study of Maria Edgeworth.* Boston: A. Williams and Company, 1882.
14. *Romilly-Edgeworth Letters 1813–1818.* Introduction

and notes by Samuel Henry Romilly. London: John
Murray, 1936.
15. Zimmern, Helen. *Maria Edgeworth*. London: W. H.
Allen and Co., 1883.

IV. CRITICISM AND COMMENT

1. Flanagan, Thomas J. *The Irish Novelists, 1800–1850*.
New York: Columbia University Press, 1959.
2. Harden, O. Elizabeth McWhorter. *Maria Edgeworth's
Art of Prose Fiction*. The Hague: Mouton, 1971.
3. Hawthorne, Mark D. *Doubt and Dogma in Maria
Edgeworth*. Gainesville: University of Florida Press,
1967.
4. Hurst, Michael. *Maria Edgeworth and the Public
Scene*. Coral Gables: University of Miami Press, 1969.
5. Newby, Percy Howard. *Maria Edgeworth*. Denver:
Swallow, 1950.
6. Newcomer, James. *Maria Edgeworth the Novelist*. Fort
Worth: Texas Christian University Press, 1967.
7. Paterson, A. *The Edgeworths: A Study of Later Eigh-
teenth Century Education*. London: W. B. Clive, 1914.